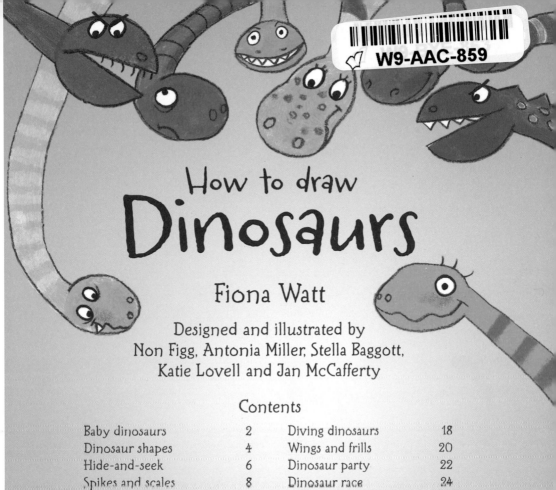

How to draw
Dinosaurs

Fiona Watt

Designed and illustrated by
Non Figg, Antonia Miller, Stella Baggott,
Katie Lovell and Jan McCafferty

Contents

Baby dinosaurs

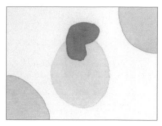

1. Mix lots of watery pale yellow paint. Then, paint a patch for the dinosaurs' nest on a large piece of white paper. Leave it to dry.

2. Mix stronger shades of orangey-yellow paint. Then, paint lots of ovals for the eggs. Make one or two of the ovals overlap.

3. Mix some orange paint, then paint a blob above an egg for a dinosaur's neck. Add an oval for a head, then let the paint dry.

Use a pen to draw lines for grass around the edge of the nest. Add some lines beneath the eggs, too.

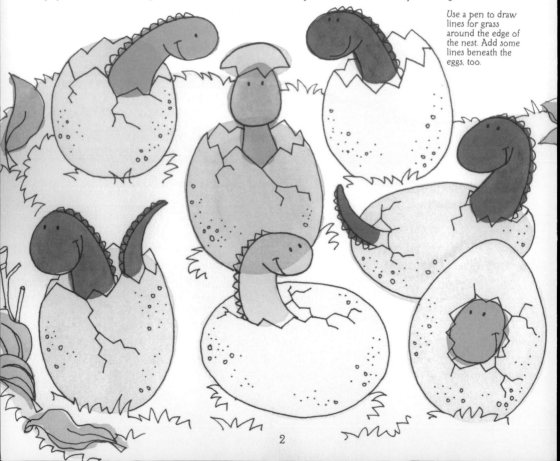

Other ideas

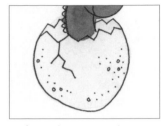

Draw a wavy line for the frill along the neck.

Use a thin felt-tip pen.

4. Draw around the head and neck, then add eyes, a mouth and a frill. Draw zigzags for the broken edge of the shell, then add the rest of the shell.

5. Then, draw zigzag lines coming from the broken edge for a crack on the shell. Add lots of little dots and circles on the shell, too.

You could paint a line for a tail, too. Make the line pointed at the tip. Draw around it in the same way as the head and neck.

You could also paint two small circles for feet beside the dinosaur's neck. Add a piece of eggshell on its head, too.

Paint a head in the middle of an egg. Draw a zigzag around the head, then add more zigzag lines for cracks on the shell.

Dinosaur shapes

This shape can be used for long-necked dinosaurs, like diplodocus and plateosaurus.

These two dinosaurs are like triceratops.

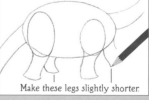

Make these legs slightly shorter.

1. For a dinosaur with a long neck, draw a large oval in the middle of your paper. Add two smaller ovals for the tops of the legs.

2. Draw a small oval for the head, above and to one side of the body. Draw a long curved neck, then add a very long tail.

3. Draw the two nearest legs coming down from the ovals you drew in step 1. Then, draw the other two legs beside them.

Draw a shape like this for a tyrannosaurus rex.

This green dinosaur is a stegosaur.

More shapes

Follow the shapes above for a dinosaur standing on its back legs. Give it very short arms.

Draw an oval for a triceratops' head at the same height as the oval for its back leg.

The body of a flying dinosaur is made up from two ovals. Its beak is a triangle.

Add spikes on its tail.

Follow these shapes to draw a dinosaur like a stegosaur. Draw diamonds on its back.

4. Draw over the outline and around the legs with a green pencil. Add an eye and a mouth. Then, erase all the pencil lines.

5. Fill in the dinosaur with watery paint. While the paint is still wet, paint some darker blobs on the back, neck and tail. Let it dry.

Hide-and-seek

Trim the pieces that overlap the edges of the paper.

1. Cut lots of pictures of exotic trees, leaves and bushes from old magazines. Look for palm trees and plants from deserts.

2. Arrange the pictures on a large piece of paper. Make some of them overlap, but leave spaces, too. Then, glue the pictures onto the paper.

3. Draw the head and neck of a tall dinosaur, peeking out over the top of one of the plants. Add eyes and a wide smiling mouth.

4. To draw a dinosaur poking out at either side of a plant, draw the head and neck at one side. Then, add the tail on the other side of the plant.

5. Draw lots of other dinosaurs hiding among the plants. You could also add some winged dinosaurs flying above the plants.

6. Fill in the dinosaurs with felt-tip pens. Decorate them with spots or stripes, too. Then, go around their outline with a darker pen.

spikes and scales

For a scene like this, paint a large hill, then fill in the sky. Cut out your dinosaurs and glue them on top.

1. Use a pencil to draw the outline of a dinosaur's body on green paper. Then, add eyes, a mouth, spikes on its tail and toenails.

Use a felt-tip pen to draw ferns around the dinosaurs.

2. Draw a bony plate in the shape of a diamond in the middle of the back. Then, draw smaller plates on both sides of the middle one.

3. Draw over your pencil lines with a felt-tip pen. Add rows of U-shaped scales along the body. Then, add teeth with correcting fluid

Fill in some of the scales.

4. Draw long lines on the bony plates with different shades of pens. Then, draw lots of little lines on the plates, spikes and toenails.

5. For a dinosaur with a frill, draw several curved lines along its back. Join the ends of the lines with shorter curved lines, like this.

6. You could also draw pointed spines along a dinosaur's back. Fill them in, then draw lots of spirals and spots on its body.

For an angry-looking dinosaur, like the one above, draw slanted eyebrows above the eyes.

Potato-printed dinosaurs

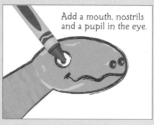

Add a mouth, nostrils and a pupil in the eye.

1. Cut a potato in half. Then, use an old spoon to spread paint on a piece of kitchen sponge cloth. This makes a good pad for printing.

2. Press the flat side of one of the pieces of potato into the paint. Press it firmly onto a piece of paper, then lift it off. Leave the paint to dry.

3. Use a green pencil or crayon to draw a neck. Then, paint a white eye. When it's dry, draw around everything with a black crayon.

This dinosaur has a painted nose and a purple pencil frill.

The pink cheeks on these dinosaurs were drawn with a pink chalk pastel.

Draw spirals in the eyes of a dizzy dinosaur.

These dinosaurs had spots or stripes added with pencils and crayons.

Overlap the first print.

4. For a dinosaur with a wide mouth, do one potato print. Then, print it again across the first print. Paint the mouth, then draw teeth.

5. For a dinosaur with an open mouth, cut a piece of potato in half again. Use one of the pieces to print the bottom, then the top, jaws.

6. You could also use one of the smaller pieces of potato to print a head like this. Draw a mouth along the straight edge.

For a picture with lots of heads, do all the potato prints first. Then, draw their necks and outline them when the paint is dry.

Hungry dinosaurs

The paint will run a little.

1. Draw a dinosaur with a long curling neck on a piece of white paper. (You could copy this one or follow steps 1-4 on pages 4-5.)

2. Dip a paintbrush into clean water, then brush it all over the paper. Dip the brush into watery green paint and blob it all over the dinosaur's body.

3. Dip the brush into the paint again and blob it over the ground beneath the dinosaur. Then, blob watery blue paint in the sky.

Use the ideas shown in this picture to draw your own dinosaur scene.

You could draw a baby dinosaur on its mother's back.

 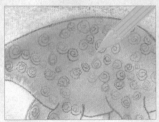 

4. When the paint is dry, draw around the dinosaur with a green pencil. Then, add an eye, nostrils and a mouth, and some toenails.

5. For the patterns on its neck, legs, body and tail, draw lots of little spirals with different shades of green and blue pencils.

6. Use a green pencil to draw some leaves in the dinosaur's mouth. Then, draw lines for the stems of ferns and add lots of looping leaves.

For a prehistoric tree, paint a brown line for the trunk and a blob for leaves on the wet paper.

Dinosaur collage

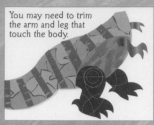

You may need to trim the arm and leg that touch the body.

1. Rip pictures of textures from old magazines. Then, draw a dinosaur's body on one of them. Cut it out and glue it onto some paper.

2. Cut strips from a different piece of magazine paper and glue them across the body. Then, cut an oval for the tummy and glue it on, too.

3. Draw arms and legs, then cut them out. Glue one arm and one leg overlapping the body. Glue on the other arm and leg just touching it.

This dinosaur has a picture of a wheel as its eye.

4. Draw two shapes for the top and bottom of the head and cut them out. Cut out a tongue, too. Glue the shapes onto the body.

5. Cut out an eye and glue it on. Cut little triangles for teeth and glue them on, too. Then, cut more triangles and glue them along the back.

6. Cut out more triangles and glue them onto the head and nose. Then, cut out some claws and glue them onto the arms and feet.

You could cut out dinosaur footprints and glue them on your picture, too.

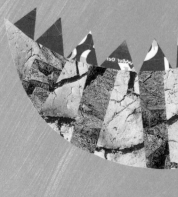

14

To paint a background like this, brush thick paint in different directions.

You could cut out lots of leaves from magazine pictures and glue them around the edges of your paper.

fingerprinted dinosaurs

Use your finger to paint the shapes.

1. Spread green paint on an old plate, then dip your finger into it. Go around and around on a piece of paper to paint a body and a head.

2. Dip your finger into the paint again and fingerprint two legs. Use a paintbrush to paint a long neck and a pointed tail.

3. When the paint is dry, fingerprint dark green spines along the dinosaur's back. Fingerprint blue spots on the body, too.

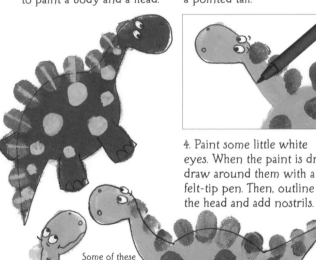

4. Paint some little white eyes. When the paint is dry draw around them with a felt-tip pen. Then, outline the head and add nostrils.

5. Draw around the body and legs, going straight across the spines on the back, not around them. Add toenails, too.

Some of these dinosaurs had spots or stripes added with a chalk pastel.

Cartoon dinosaurs

Draw dots in oval eyes for a worried look.

Draw the dot at the top of the eye to make it look scared.

A small round mouth looks surprised.

The lines across the dinosaur's neck and head make it look as if it's turning its head quickly.

These lines also help the leaves look as if they are falling.

If the dinosaur already has a long neck, draw it even longer.

1. Draw two curved lines that join up at the tail. Add an oval for the head, then draw an eye and mouth. Add a dot in the eye.

Add claws to the feet.

2. Draw two curved lines for one leg and two more small ones for the foot. Do the same for the other leg. Add spikes along its back.

Draw eyes close together and pointed teeth to make a T-rex look evil.

Fill in the dinosaur's body with a felt-tip pen.

3. Draw bent arms on the body and add fingers. Draw around the outline with a thick black felt-tip pen, then erase the pencil lines.

You could add circles on a dinosaur's back for scales.

You could add lines to make it look as if the dinosaur is running.

You could draw a shadow under the dinosaur to show that it is leaping off the ground.

Diving dinosaurs

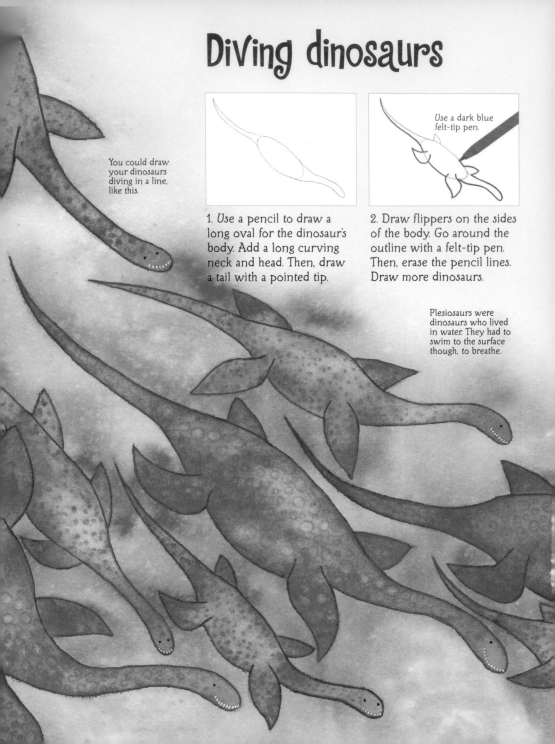

You could draw your dinosaurs diving in a line, like this.

Use a dark blue felt-tip pen.

1. *Use a pencil to draw a long oval for the dinosaur's body. Add a long curving neck and head. Then, draw a tail with a pointed tip.*

2. Draw flippers on the sides of the body. Go around the outline with a felt-tip pen. Then, erase the pencil lines. Draw more dinosaurs.

Plesiosaurs were dinosaurs who lived in water. They had to swim to the surface though, to breathe.

The ink will run.

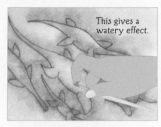

This gives a watery effect.

3. Dip a large paintbrush into clean water, then brush it all over your paper to make a watery background. Leave it to dry a little.

4. Before the paper is completely dry, dip a thinner brush into the water, then flick it to spray water all over your picture. Let it dry.

5. When your drawing is completely dry, draw over the outlines of each dinosaur again with the dark blue felt-tip pen.

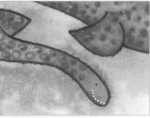

6. *Use brighter shades of blue, pink and purple felt-tip pens to draw circles all over the bodies. Then, draw some spots inside the circles*

7. Dip a thin paintbrush into clean water, then brush it over the spots and circles so that the ink runs. Try not to brush over the outlines.

8. When the ink is dry, add a row of little teeth with thick white paint or correcting fluid to each dinosaur. Then, draw their eyes.

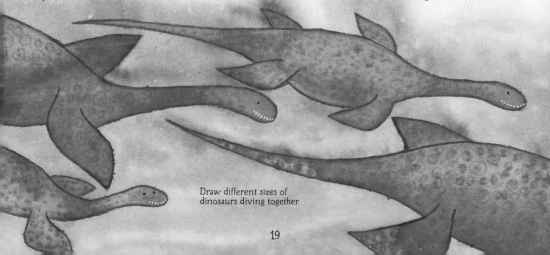

Draw different sizes of dinosaurs diving together.

You could draw some dragonflies around the pterosaurs.

Wings and frills

Let the paints run together in the middle.

Draw a wiggly line across the rocks, then add some shading.

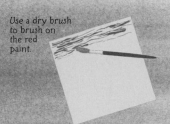

Use a dry brush to brush on the red paint.

1. Brush clean water all over a large piece of thick paper. Then, brush orange paint at the bottom and purple paint at the top.

2. When the paint is dry, paint a rocky landscape and some large stones. Draw around the shapes with a felt-tip pen.

3. To paint the paper for the dinosaurs' bodies, paint a piece of paper with yellow paint. When the paint is dry, brush red paint on top.

Make sure that the lines on the crêpe paper go in this direction, not across.

4. When the paint is dry, turn the paper over and draw the shapes of different dinosaurs, like these. Then, cut around them.

5. For a dinosaur with a frill on its back, cut a piece of crêpe paper as long as the back. Then, glue the dinosaur onto the paper.

6. Draw a line for the frill along the paper, following the shape of the dinosaur's back from its head to its tail. Cut along the line.

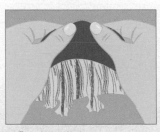

7. Gently pull the crêpe paper in several places along the back so that it stretches to make a frill. Then, draw eyes and nostrils with a pen.

8. For a flying pterosaur, cut two wings from crêpe paper. Glue them onto the body, then stretch the paper along the bottom edge of the wings.

Glue the top edge of the wings.

9. Arrange your dinosaurs on the background. Then, spread glue on their bodies and press them on. Draw some plants around them.

Dinosaur party

Draw the nose like a beak.

1. Draw a dinosaur's nose, then add a line for the bottom jaw. Draw a wavy frill at the back of the head. Add eyes and eyebrows.

2. Draw a fat body shape, including a pointed tail. Then, add three legs – the fourth one is hidden behind the body.

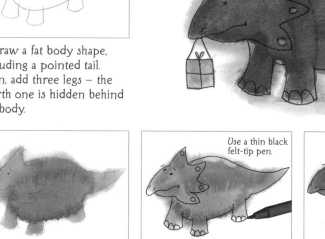

For a party feel, draw presents and balloons around the dinosaurs.

Use a thin black felt-tip pen.

3. Brush over your drawing with clean water. Blob watery paint onto the water so that it runs. Then, blob more paint along the tummy and tail.

4. When the paint is dry, draw around the head. Fill in the face and add spots on the frill. Then, draw around the body and add toenails.

5. Use a red pencil or a chalk pastel to draw a curved line around the dinosaur's body. Then, add lines all along the body, tail and legs.

Chalk pastels will give you brighter patterns than pencils (see step 5).

These dinosaurs had pale shadows painted beneath them.

More ideas

You could draw party hats on your dinosaurs. Draw a cone on top of a dinosaur's head. Add lines for a tassel at the top of the cone.

You could also draw a squeaky blower in a dinosaur's mouth. Draw curved lines around it to show that it is moving.

You could draw a ribbon tied around a dinosaur's neck. Add loops for the bow and two trailing ends of the ribbon.

Dinosaur race

The paint will run a little on the damp paper.

1. Brush clean water across a large piece of paper to make it damp. Then, brush shades of yellow paint in stripes across the paper.

2. When the paper is dry, use a pencil to draw a dinosaur. You could look back at pages 4-5 to help with the shapes.

3. Draw more dinosaurs on the paper around the first one. Make them different shapes - it doesn't matter if they overlap each other.

The diagonal lines and splattered paint make the dinosaurs look as if they are running.

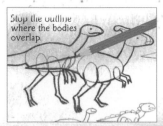

Stop the outline where the bodies overlap.

4. Draw around a dinosaur with a red pencil. Then, draw around another one in purple, avoiding the lines where the dinosaurs overlap.

Use two shades of pencils.

5. Erase all the pencil lines. Then, to make the dinosaurs look as if they are moving, fill them in using lots of diagonal lines.

6. Dip a paintbrush into brown paint, then flick your finger across the bristles to splatter paint around the dinosaurs' feet.

Prehistoric swamp

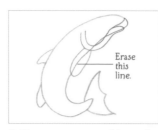

1. Use a pencil to draw a curved body of a prehistoric fish in the middle of a large piece of paper. Add three fins and a tail.

Erase this line.

2. Draw two curved lines for the jaws. Then, erase the line of the body across the fin and jaws. Go over all your lines with a blue pencil.

Add some pointed teeth.

3. Draw an eye, then add large scales around it. Draw lines on the fins and the end of the tail. Then, fill in the tail with lots of scales.

4. Draw another fish curving around the first one. Go over the outline with a red pencil, then fill in the scales as you did before.

5. Draw a fish with a triangular head. Add a spine and wavy lines along its back. Then, draw curved lines below it for sand.

6. Draw smaller fish, worms and a water snake to fill the spaces around your fish. Add patterns and scales along their backs.

7. For the top of the water, use a blue pencil to draw wavy lines across the first fish you drew. Draw yellow lines above the fish, for sand.

8. Draw two more swamp creatures on the sand. Add legs, scales and spines. Draw a bug and dragonflies in the spaces between them.

9. Use different shades of watery paint to fill in the prehistoric creatures. Paint the water and sky in blue, and the sand in yellow.

Don't fill in the dragonflies' wings.

Tyrannosaurus rex

This background was painted after the dinosaurs were finished.

1. Draw a small oval for the dinosaur's head. Then, draw a bigger oval for its body. Draw it below the head, at an angle, like this.

2. Draw two curved lines joining the head and the body, for the neck. Then, draw a tail curving out behind the body.

For a dinosaur bending down, like this one, draw the ovals for its head and body in a straight line.